Erie & Spuds

Matthew Rapuano

Copyright © Matthew Rapuano 2024

All Rights Reserved

No part of this publication may be reproduced, distributed, or transmitted in any form or by any means, including photocopying, recording, or other electronic or mechanical methods, without the author's prior written permission, except in the case of brief quotations embodied in critical reviews and certain other non-commercial uses permitted by copyright law. For permission requests, please get in touch with the author.

Hello, I am Erie, and I am a blue rabbit with a black fedora hat. I am here to tell you a story. A story about a friend of mine I met many months ago.

It was a nice, calm, relaxing Sunday afternoon. And I had decided to take a nice stroll down the road to sightsee around me. It was a very standard Sunday...

On my walk, I noticed two yellow ears popping out of a hole in the ground. It caught my interest, and I assumed it must have been a fellow bunny rabbit digging. I took a look...

It was a yellow bunny rabbit, and he was just sitting there quietly with sweat dripping down his face. I thought I would talk to him.

In a very calm manner, the yellow bunny rabbit simply responded,

"Yes, I am fine."

I decided to ask him, "Do you need help getting out?"

I then pulled him out by the ears with ease. The bunny rabbit was rather light for a big rabbit like myself. I felt then I would place him down and talk.

I decided to get to know him, and I had a pleasant talk with him.
I asked what his name was, and what was it?

"I'm Spuds! I'm called that because...well, I love potatoes."

He ate the potato instantly, and Spuds seems like an easy-going fellow. And thus, from here on, we had our adventures together.

I'd say after about a week or so, I invited Spuds to my house to hang out. I thought we could have some fun things to do. What kind of things, you may ask?

We started making some food! As Spuds mentioned, he really likes potatoes. To the point where it was really potatoes themselves that he would usually eat alone.
I felt the little guy could try new things.

Spuds would only really eat raw potatoes. I think it's time I help him try different things. But first, why not try mashed potatoes instead of a normal potato?

The smell certainly caught his attention and next thing you know...

He had eaten the whole container. Oh well, glad he enjoyed it.

We played a game of chess, and we ended up in a draw.

And then I tried doing a handstand with him. It was amazing, he was able to do one on his ears.

I even decided to show him how to go fishing, as he never done it before. Although, frankly, we probably wouldn't catch any fish in this area.

He came walking by, but I noticed something different about him.

"Spuds?" I asked. "Are you feeling alright? You seem to be acting a bit, well, funny. And this is the first time I've seen you today."

"Well, I have been shaving my whiskers off lately. I thought it'd make me look good."

If I'm being honest, I think I've only seen another rabbit do that once in my life. I wonder if Spuds knows the importance of whiskers. I decided to explain it to him.

"Spuds, dear bud! You shouldn't shave off your whiskers! Many of us animals need to have our whiskers on our faces." I continued lecturing Spuds about the mistake he made. I almost took it that he can be a bit of a risk-taker.

"They help us not bump into things. Without mine, I could bump into a light pole," said Erie. "Whiskers are like our special sensors. They let us know when something is close by, even if we can't see it. So, we can move around safely and find our way."

After hearing this, I had to help out Spuds. The first step was to address the issue. Now, the next step is to help him... but how?

Actually, the more I think about it, I realize I haven't seen my good buddy Wilbur in a while. I think I will pay him a visit with Spuds.

Wilbur is a librarian at a library. He's one of my closest friends, and I feel he may be able to help us. Also, I just realized the building almost looks like his head.

I thought I would open the door for Spuds.

I forgot for a second about his whiskers, and he hit the wall.

"Sorry, Spuds!" I shouted.

Wilbur would spend a few hours every Sunday working on some paperwork. However, he would leave the door unlocked if someone wanted to stop by.

"Wilbur! It's Erie! How are you?"

"Erie! Old pal! Glad to see you!"

I proceeded to ask Wilbur, "We have a problem. My friend Spuds here cut off his whiskers. How do we handle an issue like this?"

Wilbur took a moment to look at the little guy without his whiskers on his face.

Wilbur proceeded to say, "Ah! I have a book that can help you with whiskers."

"I can also tell you more about your situation, as I have read many books myself. But hold on just a second while I go get it."

We watched him go up that ladder. Wilbur has always been a very fast dog.

He pulled a book from the shelf that was simply titled Whiskers.

"That book has everything you need to know about whiskers," Wilbur said. He gave us the book for free.

Wilbur continued, "Now, it may take weeks, maybe months, for the whiskers to grow back all the way, Spuds."

As Wilbur discussed this, Spuds just stood there and didn't notice until now something about Wilbur.

Even dogs seem to have whiskers on their faces.

Spuds and I then left the library as I waved goodbye to my old friend Wilbur. Spuds tried balancing the book in between his ears.

Oops, I forgot about Spuds again. "Sorry again, Spuds" I said out of embrassment. He bumped into the wall, once more.

Although Spuds reading the book wasn't a problem for him, it also meant he didn't see where he was going. So, I thought I would help him.

I tried to be his guide, placing my hands on his shoulders. I just felt bad for the times before when he had hit the wall.

I successfully brought Spuds home. He has a nice little place that is perfectly convenient.

And you know, the thing with us rabbits is that we leave our mothers at a rather young age, so we head into the world not knowing as much. I think whiskers are one thing Spuds didn't get to learn much about.

Spuds then dropped the book right on his face. He seemed to have remembered something important, which I initially thought was because he was getting tired.

"Erie!" he shouted. The funny thing is,
I never told him my name;
he overheard it when I talked to Wilbur.

"I still have the whiskers that I shaved off!" Spuds exclaimed.

Huh...

I was a little dumbfounded. I thought he would have thrown them away. Then again, I was curious about where this was going.

He quickly retrieved them from his room, and they were in a small plastic bag.

Well, I was certainly weirded out by that. What was he planning to do with them?

What Spuds was trying to do was simply put them back on his face. But sadly...

When he tried to put the whiskers on, they just fell right off his face. I had to break the news to him.

This must have been the first time I'd seen Spuds so down. I thought I'd cheer him up by reminding him of something.

"Erie, I feel so foolish having done this," Spuds said.

I proceeded to ask him, "It's okay, Spuds. We all make mistakes. But tell me, do you know what whiskers can do?"

"Why, yes! They can be glued back on! Let me get the glue!"

I stopped him. "Hold on, Spuds! That's not what I meant!"

"Spuds, bud, listen. Remember what Wilbur said: your whiskers will grow back, but it will take time. Weeks, maybe months."

I think I got him to understand now. I wanted to reassure him of something, though.

"I will be your guide for the next few weeks, and I'm sure people where you work will guide you, too."

He seemed to have appreciated that.

So, I started staying with Spuds

on the weekends.

At his job, Spuds works as a gardener on a farm. A coworker of his was very supportive and stood by Spuds throughout this time.

Then, one morning, I walked down the sidewalk to Spuds' place.

And who did I see coming?

It was Spuds. And wouldn't you know it, his whiskers had fully grown back.

Since it was Saturday and I hadn't seen him since the previous Sunday, it was a pleasant surprise.

Needless to say, I was very happy for him.

"Well, congratulations, Spuds!"

That afternoon, I went to the end of a dock on a lake with Spuds to help him with his fishing skills.

"Well, Spuds, I'm sure you have learned a lesson from this, haven't you?"

"Yep! Don't shave."

Well, good enough, I suppose.
Though I should also warn
him about scissors.

Just then, my friend Ralph,
the tabby cat, came by and said hi.

"Hi, guys! Fishing?"

"Hello, Ralph! Yes, we are. What have you been up to?"

"I cut my claws, something I've never done before!"

"Ralph! You shouldn't do that because y—"

....

Here we go again.

The end.

About the Author

Matt Rap is a ginger cartoonist who, outside of other activities, tends to spend his free time working on artwork. He creates a variety of art including animations that can be found on Youtube as well as books. He is one to change up what he chooses to create, whether they are for kids or for everyone to enjoy. His work may be found online by the name "Gingercartoonist".

Made in United States
North Haven, CT
16 February 2025